W9-BNQ-433

WINDMILL BOOKS
New York

Published in 2016 by **Windmill Books**, an Imprint of Rosen Publishing
29 East 21st Street, New York, NY 10010

Models made by Fiona Gowen.

Images on pages 4 and 5 © shutterstock.com

Cataloging-in-Publication Data
Reynolds, Toby.
Junk modeling / by Toby Reynolds.
p. cm. — (Mini artists)
Includes index.
ISBN 978-1-4777-5670-6 (pbk.)
ISBN 978-1-4777-5669-0 (6 pack)
ISBN 978-1-4777-5572-3 (library binding)
1. Handicraft — Juvenile literature.
2. Refuse as art material — Juvenile literature.
I. Reynolds, Toby. II. Title.
TT160.R434 2016
745.5—d23

Manufactured in the United States of America
CPSIA Compliance Information: Batch # WS15WM: For Further Information contact Rosen Publishing, New York, New York at 1-800-237-9932

Contents

Getting Started

The projects in this book use lots of art materials that you will already have at home. Any missing materials can be found in art shops and stationery stores.

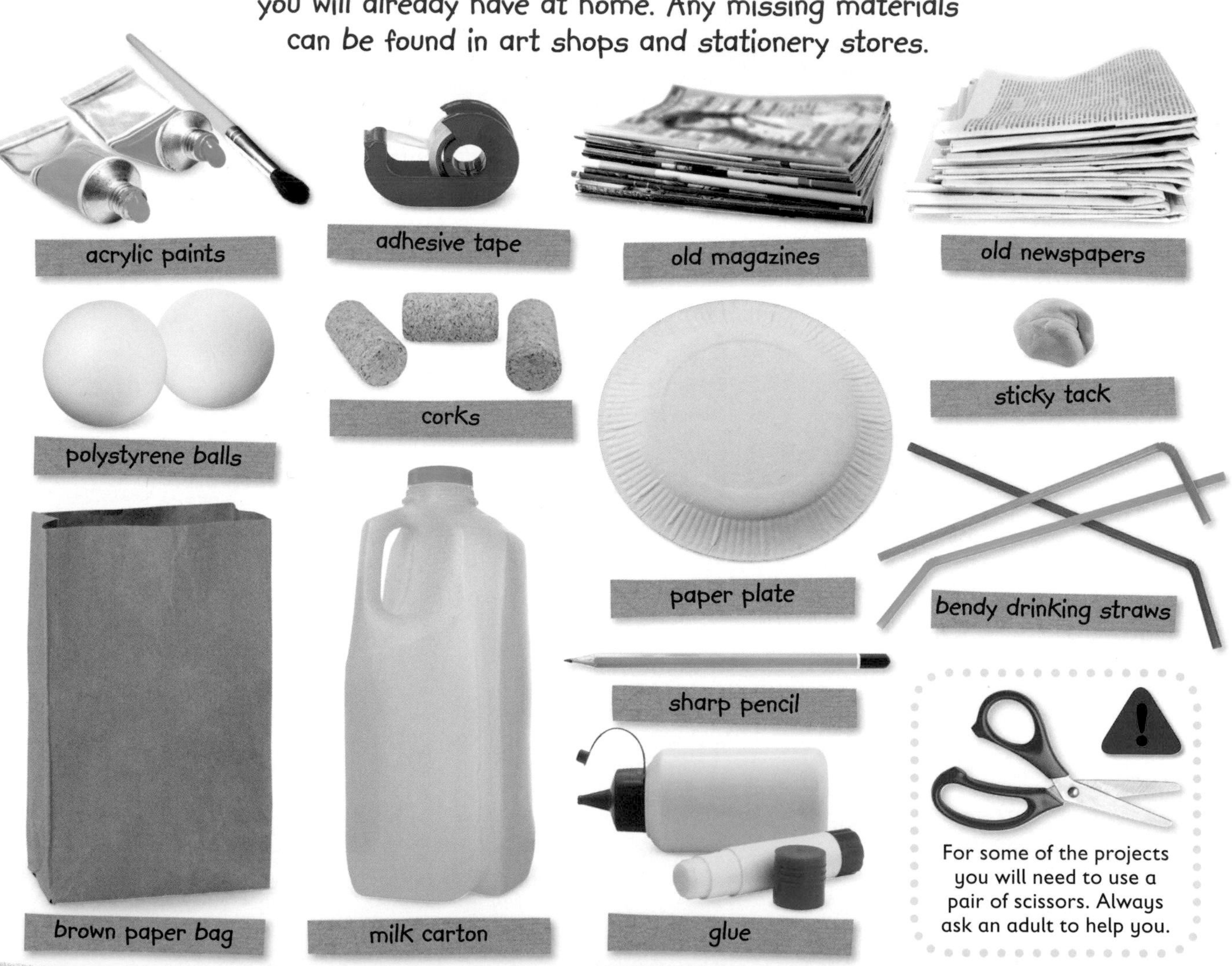

For some of the projects you will need to use a pair of scissors. Always ask an adult to help you.

Handy Hint

Always keep some old clothes that can be cut up and used for craft projects. It's fun to recycle clothing into something new!

Here is a selection of paper and card stock you can use to complete the puppet projects.

Rolling Racers

To make these racing cars, you will need toilet rolls, paints, paper fastners, paper, card stock, and a felt-tip pen.

1 You can start making your racer by painting the inside and outside of a toilet roll any color you like.

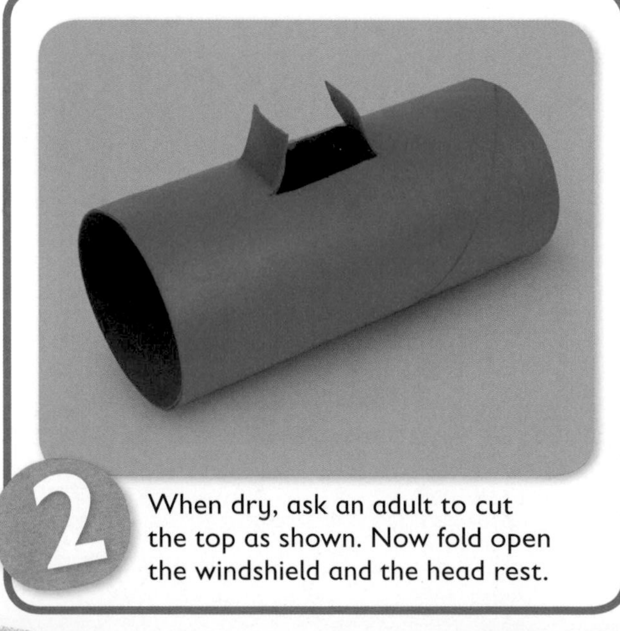

2 When dry, ask an adult to cut the top as shown. Now fold open the windshield and the head rest.

3 Cut a circle from colored paper. Write your racing car's number on the paper and then glue it into place.

4 Now you can make the wheels for your car. Cut four big circles from card stock and paint them black.

5 Ask an adult to help you push a paper fastener into the middle of each wheel and attach them to the racing car.

6 You can make some more racing cars using different colors and numbers. Now it's time to race!

Crazy Caterpillar

To make this caterpillar model you will need a large egg carton, paint, paper, and a pipe cleaner.

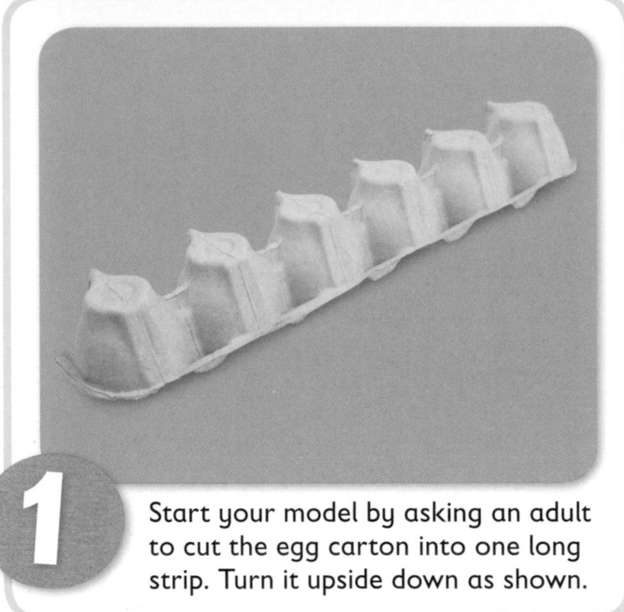

1 Start your model by asking an adult to cut the egg carton into one long strip. Turn it upside down as shown.

2 Next you can paint the carton a bright color. Now you will have to wait patiently for the paint to dry.

3 When it is ready, ask an adult to poke two holes in the front of the carton. These are for the antennae.

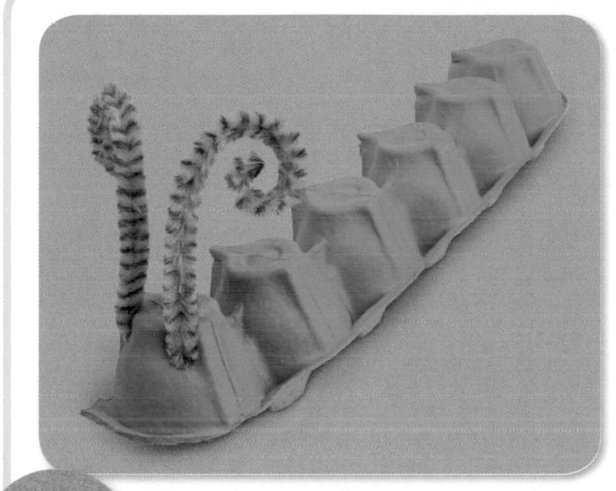

4 Thread a pipe cleaner in one of the holes and back out through the other. Curl the ends as shown.

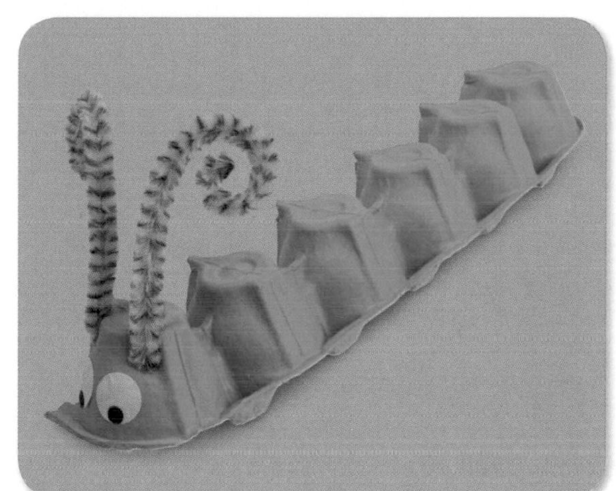

5 Cut two white paper circles for eyes and glue them to the caterpillar's face. Glue black paper circles on top.

6 Now you can make some friends for your caterpillar. Try painting each of your caterpillars a different color.

Paper Bag House

To make this model house you will need a paper bag, colored paper, old newspapers, and a felt-tip pen.

1 Start your house model by filling the paper bag with scrunched up sheets from some old newspapers.

2 Push the newspapers into the bag and carefully fold the top of the bag. Glue or staple the bag closed.

3 Now take three colored squares of paper and glue them to the front of the bag for the door and windows.

4 Use a piece of colored paper to form a roof for the house. Fold the roof and glue or staple it into place.

5 Use some colored paper to create a chimney on the top of the roof. Glue the chimney onto the roof.

6 Finally use a felt-tip pen to add some tile details to the roof. Now you can make a street of paper bag houses!

Milk Carton House

For this fun house you will need a plastic milk carton, paint, crêpe or tissue paper, colored paper, and glue.

1 To begin your milk carton model, ask an adult to cut a large hole into the side of a clean milk carton.

2 Ask an adult to now cut two small square holes in the carton. These will be the windows of the house.

3 Now you can begin decorating the house. First paint the inside walls of the house in any color you like.

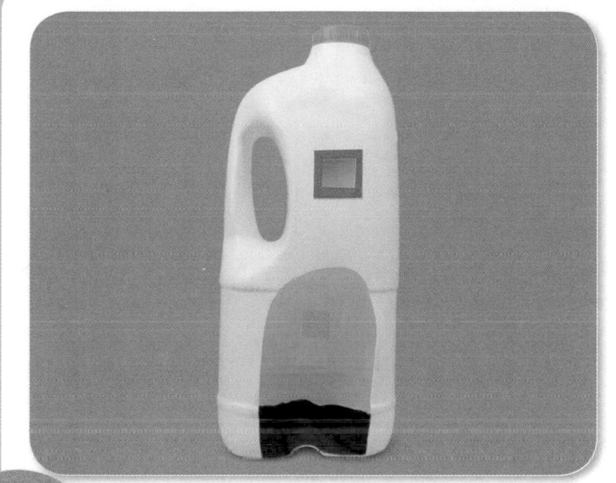

4 Glue crêpe or tissue paper to the floor of the house and strips of colored paper around the windows for frames.

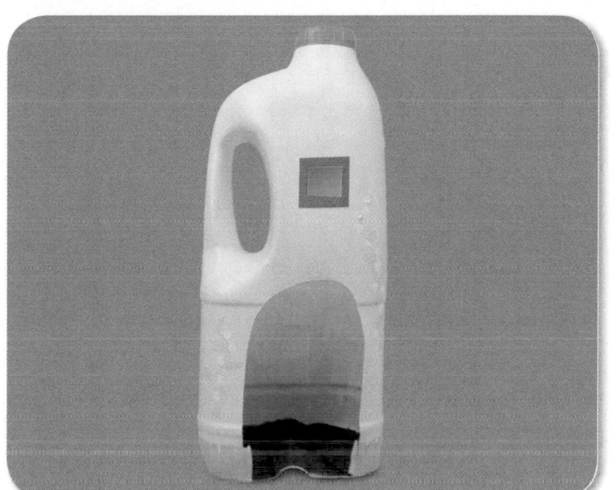

5 Decorate the outside of the house with green paper for grass. You can paint plants and flowers on as well.

6

Finish your house by filling it with curtains, a television, and some furniture made from paper or card stock.

Fire Engine

For this fire engine you will need a cardboard box, paints, paper, card stock, glue, and a pipe cleaner.

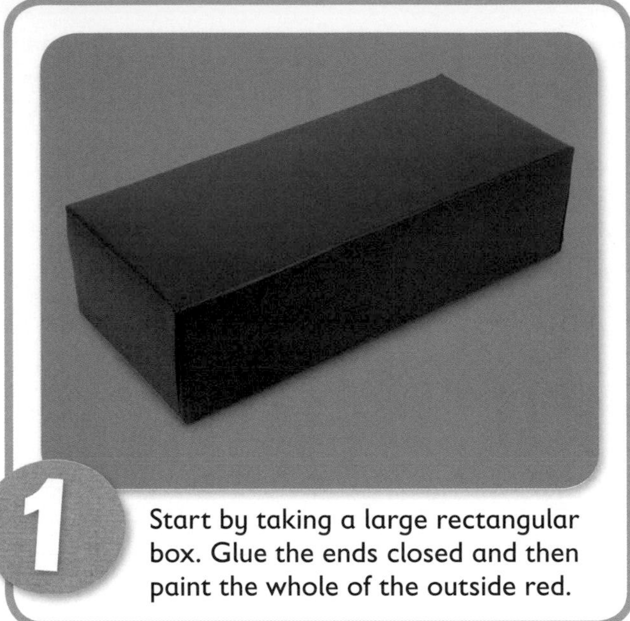

1 Start by taking a large rectangular box. Glue the ends closed and then paint the whole of the outside red.

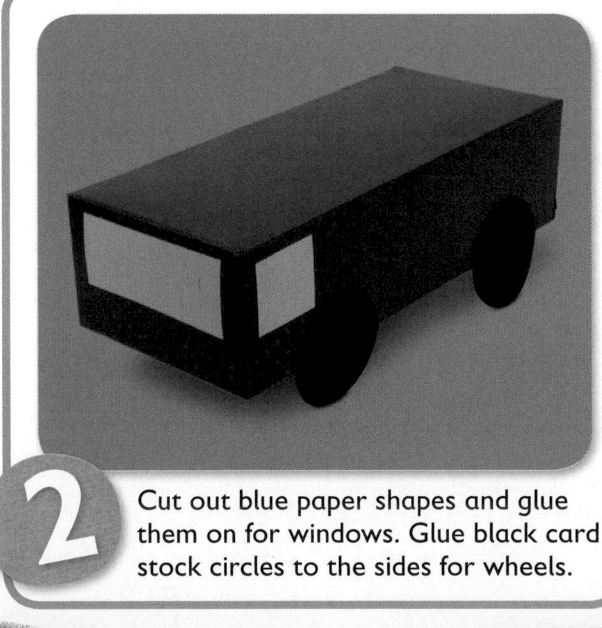

2 Cut out blue paper shapes and glue them on for windows. Glue black card stock circles to the sides for wheels.

3 Now cut two yellow circles for headlights and some gray strips for the grill. Glue them into place.

4 To make the ladder on top of the fire engine cut out black strips of card stock and glue them to the roof.

5 Glue a gray rectangle of paper for the side panel. Curl a pipe cleaner and glue it to the engine for the hose.

6 Now you can try making all different types of emergency vehicles using this method.

Super Snowman

To make this snowman you will need newspapers, a white trash bag, a hat, a scarf, and black card stock.

1 Start to make your snowman by placing scrunched up sheets of newspaper into a white trash bag.

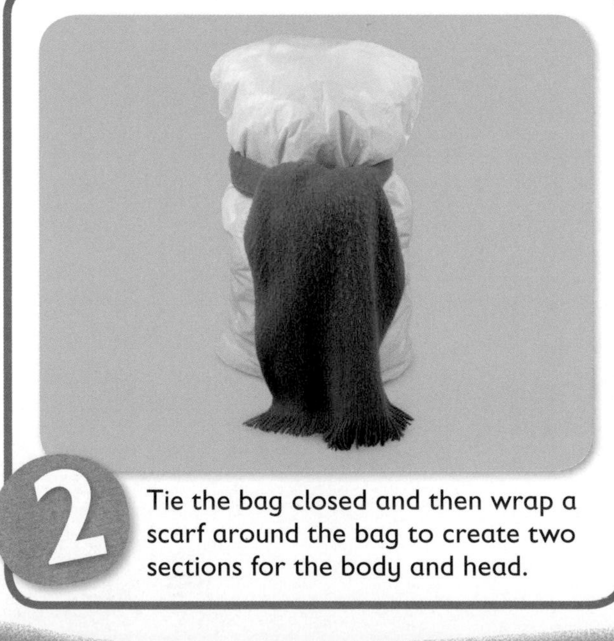

2 Tie the bag closed and then wrap a scarf around the bag to create two sections for the body and head.

3 Now you will need to find a fun hat for your snowman to wear. Place the hat on top of your snowman's head.

4 Cut black card stock shapes for the eyes and mouth. You can glue these into place on the snowman's face.

5 Using the same black card stock, cut two shapes for the snowman's arms and hands. Glue these into place.

6 Now your snowman is complete, you can make some friends for him!

Tiny Tree Frog

For this frog you need small boxes, red bottle tops, straws, paint, black paper, glue, and sticky tack.

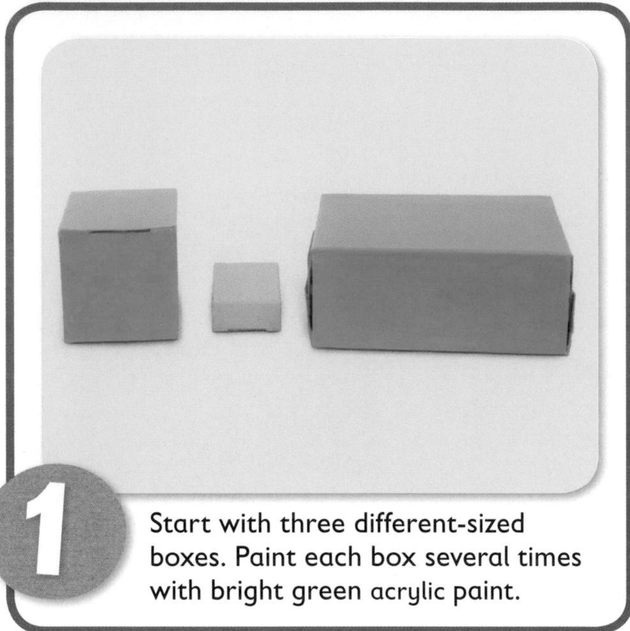

1 Start with three different-sized boxes. Paint each box several times with bright green acrylic paint.

2 After the green paint has dried, you can glue each of the three boxes together into a line as shown here.

3 Now use two red bottle tops for eyes. Use small pieces of sticky tack to keep them in position on the frog.

4 Ask an adult to make holes in the side and bottom of the largest box. Insert lengths of straws for the legs.

5 Using a black felt-tip pen, carefully draw a wide mouth onto the front and two sides of the tree frog's head.

6 Finish your frog by gluing a thin strip of black paper onto each of the bottle top eyes to give him character.

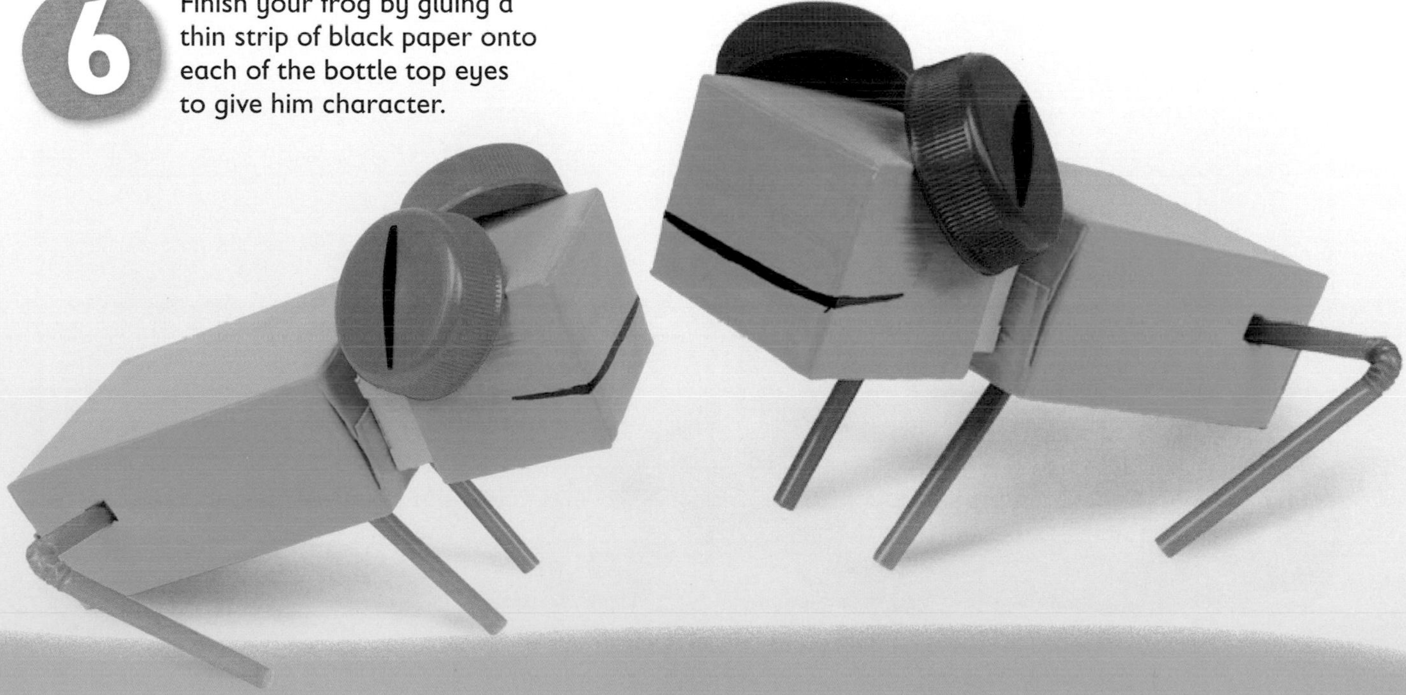

Baby Tiger Cub

For this tiger cub you need a toilet roll, a polystyrene ball, corks, card stock, paint, paper, glue, and tissue paper.

1 Start by painting the toilet roll, polystyrene ball, and corks with several coats of orange acrylic paint.

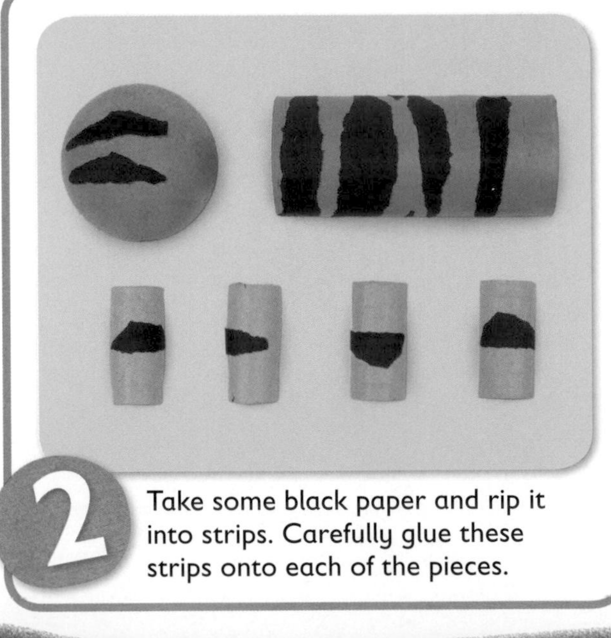

2 Take some black paper and rip it into strips. Carefully glue these strips onto each of the pieces.

3 Now put your tiger cub together. Glue the cork legs and polystyrene head onto the toilet roll body.

4 Cut these two shapes from orange card stock for the ears. Fold the ears and then glue them onto the head.

5 Glue paper eyes onto the face. Use a felt-tip pen to draw circles on the eyes, then add a nose and whiskers.

6 To finish your tiger, use twisted strips of orange and black tissue paper to make a tail. Glue the tail onto the tiger's body.

Paper Flowers

For these flowers you will need old magazines, adhesive tape, a green straw, a sharp pencil, and glue.

1 Start by folding old magazine pages in half and then in half again. Cut a petal shape from the corner.

2 Open the flower to see the petals. Repeat the first step three times, using different sizes and colors.

3 Lightly glue the four sets of petals on top of each other. Use a sharp pencil to make a small hole in the middle.

4 Take a green bendy straw and push the short end through the hole in the center of your paper flower.

5 Cut the end of the straw into four separate pieces. Fold them back and tape onto the front of the flower.

6 Once you have mastered making this pretty paper flower, you could make enough to fill a vase!

Glossary

character features marking and often individualizing a person or figure

material something used to make something else, such as a fabric

polystyrene a rigid plastic used in foams and molded products

stationery materials for writing or typing

windshield a transparent screen (such as glass) in front of people in a vehicle

Index

Further Reading

Jones, Jen. *Cool Crafts with Newspapers, Magazines, and Junk Mail.* Mankato, MN: Capstone Press, 2011.

Llimos, Anna. *Earth-Friendly Crafts from Recycled Stuff in 5 Easy Steps.* New York: Enslow, 2013.

Websites

For web resources related to the subject of this book, go to:
www.windmillbooks.com/weblinks and select this book's title.